Come, Boy!
Train Your Dog to Come Every Time

MICHELLE HUNTTING

COME, BOY!

Cover Designed by: Victoria Davies &
Ashley Thompson

Cover Photos by: Amber Craig

Hair & Makeup: Karen Cribb

Editor: Gayle Davis

ISBN-13: 978-1493525898
ISBN-10: 1493525891

Disclaimer

This book has been written with the intention of providing information, entertainment, and education to pet owners and trainers. It is written with the understanding that pet owners will use their judgment or employ a skilled professional dog trainer or animal behaviorist for additional assistance if needed.

Training doesn't come without risks. The author and the contributors to this book will not be held liable for any caused or alleged damage to result directly or indirectly from the information found in this book.

This book has been written with the greatest degree of accuracy possible, but there may be unforeseen and unintentional mistakes in the content. Michelle Huntting, and other contributors, will have neither liability nor responsibility to any person or entity with respect to any damage caused, any loss or alleged damage to have been caused, directly or indirectly by the information contained in this book.

MICHELLE HUNTTING

DEDICATION

To my Boy, Morgan, and Miss Belle

CONTENTS

PREFACE

Come, Boy! is a work of love for my own training students as well as pet owners everywhere who are struggling with establishing the behavior of *come*. This book was borne from my experience of nearly a decade of training single and multiple dog homes as well as my own family dogs. I know personally the agonizing fear that strikes me when a gate is accidentally left open and I have a missing dog, or in my experience as a trainer, observing a dog that bolts from the front door.

Come is the most important cue to strongly establish with your dogs because it could very well save his life.

My goal was to assemble an easy-to-follow manual that any pet owner or trainer could immediately implement. If you follow the steps in *Come, Boy!*, within four weeks, you should have a strongly established *come* behavior.

The book details the three pillars of establishing *come*. Also included are chapters on multiple dog training, whistle and vibration collar training, as well as a chapter for training a recall for deaf dogs, written by Christina Lee, owner of Deaf Dogs Rock.

To facilitate the reader, the manual style of *Come, Boy!* enables you to seek the chapter that best addresses the immediate issue you are struggling with.

However, with the behavior of *come*, it is important that you build the foundational skills before adding more difficult tasks such as multiple dogs, distractions, or whistle training.

Please note that throughout the book I refer to the masculine gender only. I did this for two reasons: One, I grew up with traditional English grammar, and use of the masculine is simply more natural for me. Two, it was just easier than dealing with the awkward he/she combo. Know that I am equally supportive of both genders.

Enjoy the ride! Your reading experience and implementation of the suggested methods should help you to establish not only the expected outcome of a positive recall but also a stronger, more intimate relationship with your canine companion.

ACKNOWLEDGMENTS

I have been incredibly blessed in this season of life with my friends and my southern family. I love you with all of my heart and am grateful for each and every one of you. This book was written with your inspiration and help in my daily life.

Thank you to those that helped contribute directly to this book: Gayle Davis who is much more than an editor and to Christina Lee for your contribution on recalls for deaf dogs. Thank you to those that contributed photos: Robert & Felicity Sanders, Cheryl Kenyon, Verena Thompson, Miranda Vallade, Renea Dahms, Amber Craig, and Jaclyn Bicicchi.

"Our prime purpose in this life is to help others."
-Dalai Lama

CHAPTER 1
INTRODUCTION

Imagine your dog ran through the doorway when you opened it to pick up a package that was just delivered, and he ran out into the front yard. Panic strikes. You are nearly paralyzed with fear that your beloved pet will take off on you, or, worse yet, run into traffic. Your thoughts race: *Oh my gosh! Cars are going to come!* Praying he will listen, you yell your dog's name. What happens?

A solid *come* to your call is the fervent desire of every pet owner. What if I told you that if you follow the exercises in this book, even if all three of your dogs got out into the front yard, they would listen and come back to you? Wouldn't that be an awesome and worthwhile invitation to following the protocols I suggest in the upcoming pages?!

As part of my training with my own dogs, I worked hard on recalls (*come*) with all three individually, then collectively. Every day we did sessions for several months, and it has been so worth the work that I invested. The exercises that I put together in this book will take 10-15 minutes per day. If you work on the exercises five days a week for four weeks and then after that review with your dog two-three days a week, you will continue to see a solid *come.*

When I work with dogs or just visit with my friend's dogs, I know that the number one cue I can count on their knowing is *sit.* In fact, there was a time that I was pet sitting when the dog showed signs that he was about to bite me, but I cued a *sit,* and he immediately came out of bite mode and sat. It's almost funny how strong the *sit* cue is for dogs. Why do you think that is? The number one reinforced cue in the dog world by every single pet owner is *sit.* When we pull the dog treat out of our beautifully decorated dog cookie jar, what do we ask for? That's right! I would bet money on it that you ask your dog for a *sit.* Hence, we continuously reinforce *sit,* likely at the expense of other training cues.

So, let's retrain ourselves! This is not easy to do but very possible. Stop asking for *sit* when you pull out the treats; instead ask *come.*

Though *sit* is the number one command dogs know, *come* is the number one most important cue he should know because it could very well save his life. In order for this cue to be as strong as *sit,* it needs to be reinforced and revisited often.

On a personal level, as I have entered my 30's, I have become more active, more health minded, and over-all more conscious of my body. I honestly didn't give much thought as to what foods I put into my body, the amount of sleep I received, or the amount of exercise I got when I was in my early and even mid 20's. That shifted for me when I realized that I only had one body and needed to take care of myself. With this new change of life for myself, I started doing yoga and weight lifting on a weekly basis. I notice that if I take a week or more off, my muscles begin to feel "soft." My muscles haven't lost all shape in that amount of time, of course, but they certainly don't feel as strong as they do when I am working them at least 2-3 times during the week.

This weakening is what happens with the *come* cue for your dog. If you aren't revisiting it frequently (on a weekly basis), your dog's response will begin to get weak. The longer you go without reinforcing it, the weaker it becomes just like unworked muscles.

Sit for dogs is the strongest cue because it's daily visited or he daily receives "workouts" with this cue, so begin to challenge yourself to give him "workouts" with the cue *come.*

> *Challenge yourself to work on* come *for 30 days, and after that continue to revisit this cue with your dog at least 2-3 times a week.*

Let's think about the cue *come*. This cue requires your dog to leave whatever item he was focused on, turn to look at you, and then move toward you. Essentially there are three pillars in training *come.*

Eye Contact   Leave it!   Movement toward you

Three pillars for a solid recall:
- Eye contact
- Leave it!
- Movement toward you

In this book I have included all the exercises to successfully teach your dog the skills, information on all the tools needed for *come,* and trouble shooting. Good luck and happy training!

CHAPTER 2
YOUR TOOLS

When working on the *come* cue, there are a few tools that you will need.

Drop Line
A drop line can be a long nylon leash or a rope that you can have dragging on the ground as a safety precaution as you are working on your recall skills.

You can order a fancy drop line from online (www.sitstay.com), or you can make your own. You will need a 15 ft rope with a regular dog leash clip on the end. You are welcome to make knots at intervals along the rope so that if your dog does start to run, you can step on the line without it slipping through under your foot. If you have a petite breed, a smaller dog leash clip and rope is a must, and 10 feet will work great.

Treat Tote (Bait Bag)
A treat tote, also known as a bait bag, is another important tool in your training arsenal. My favorites are Premium's® treat pouch or Outward Hound®. I

like these pouches as they can be easily opened or closed, and I can quickly move the position of the treat pouch around to have it on my right or left side or behind me. There are many other similar brands available. These products can be found at your local pet food store as well as websites like www.amazon.com or www.sitstay.com.

I have one caution with using a bait bag. First, it's important that you randomly use this tool as you train because if you *always* use the bait bag, your dog will begin to realize that when the bait bag is on, it's training time, and that will become the only time he listens to you.

When I work on recalls, I will have treats hidden in different places, in pockets, for example, and randomly use my bait bag.

Food

When establishing the behavior of *come*, treats are a very important tool. Chapter 4 in this book discusses how to use your treats properly. I know it may be silly to think treats would be a part of the tool box, but they are a very important element to training *come*.

As a mother of toddler twins, I am currently going through the potty training process with them. Let me just say that it is much easier to train two puppies than two little boys. If you are a parent, then you are familiar with the desperation of getting your child to figure out that "potties" go in the big boy (or girl) toilet. Parents have used many of their own tools as reinforcers. Yesterday a father was sharing with me that his daughter, whom he was in the process of potty training, was crazy about chocolates, so he used those as his reinforcer. However, she quickly figured out how to "beat the system." She would hastily sit on the potty, hop off without so much as a tinkle, and run out to him with her hand held out awaiting her precious piece of milk chocolate.

Quite obviously we would never give chocolates to our dogs, but I hope that you are beginning to see my point: dogs will work for something that they love. They will quickly come when they know something is in it for them. However, typically, this is the point when my training students comment, "Well, Michelle, I want to be such a great leader in my pack that my dogs come without any food."

My answer to them is that treats will facilitate your leadership skills. Giving your dog something that he wants after he comes accomplishes several objectives:

- Reinforces the desired behavior
- Increases the speed of the desired behavior
- Creates a positive feeling with the word *come*
- Creates a reliable behavior
- Builds a stronger bond between you and your dog
- Builds a strong motivation to come to you

The Marker

One of the method styles I reference throughout this book with many training exercises is a marker based teaching method. If you've ever gone to Sea World®, you will see the trainer blow the whistle and then throw a fish. What the trainer is doing is using a marker training method with the whistle as the marker. When the dolphin, for example, jumps and that's what the trainer wants, the trainer blows the whistle (marks) and then throws a fish (reinforces). I use the same method with dogs. Anything can be used as the marker sound (or, in case of a deaf dog, a hand signal). The marker can be a specific word (for example, "yep"), a whistle, or most popularly, a clicker. A clicker is a small metal strip in a plastic box, which, when you push the button, makes a distinct sound.

For the exercises in this book specifically, I would encourage you to use a verbal word and a clicker. The reason is simple: they are the most practical for the exercises that will be conducted. Verbal markers are great when you are on the move, and the clicker is ideal for really fast behaviors that would physically be easier for you to quickly push the clicker than to mark with your word.

When using a maker method, you mark the desired behavior, and you reinforce the behavior with food, petting, praise, etc., anything that your dog will respond favorably to.

For example, if you wanted me to sit in a specific chair, you would click the moment my bottom touched the chair, and then you would hand me $50 for sitting.

Because you handed me the $50, the likelihood of my going back to sit in the chair has greatly increased. When you marked my behavior with a click, I knew specifically what you wanted.

With this method you did not use the mark (like pointing a remote and pressing the "on" button) to get a *sit*. Instead, you used the mark to establish the *sit* and reinforced it with money. So, for dogs we would mark, for example, as soon as his bottom touches the floor to establish a *sit* and then reinforce with a tasty treat after we click.

Once he is offering the behavior all the time without any prompting, you know that you've established a *sit* behavior. The next step is to add a name, or what trainers call a cue, to the behavior such as the word "sit." When training puppies, I like to add a non-verbal cue which could be your hand motioning up as you say "sit." After you practice this procedure for several days, you will then ask for a *sit* and see what your dog does. If he sits, great! Mark, treat, and praise!

Just as I occasionally hear objections in other areas of dog training, I hear concerns expressed about clicker training.

Following is a list of these concerns, and my response to them:

Concern: I will always be walking around with a clicker in my hand. This idea is false. If you use clicker training correctly, you will establish a desired behavior, name it (give it a cue), and then fade (withdraw) the click from your arsenal of tools as soon as the dog is able to follow the cue without the sound of the click.

Concern: My dog will only work for the food. This is also false. After you start using the clicker and find out how much fun it is and what a reliable method of training it is, you will be addicted and so will your dog. It will become a game to him, and the reward for him will become the sound of the click rather than the food.

The beauty of using the clicker is it's a hands-off method that helps your dog learn to think on his own. He wants to work for you, and he is excited about doing so. He soon starts to work, not for the food, but for the sound of the click. The food becomes a bonus.

Just as the clicker is faded, treats will be faded as well. Random reinforcement (food, praise, walk, toy, game, etc.), however, is never faded.

Concern: The click cues the dog so, in other words, I click and he sits. I have observed trainers using the clicker as a cue, for example, rather than the actual *come* command. This isn't "wrong," but the click is not being used as a marker. A marker is not a cue. A marker is the signal that what my dog just did in that moment is exactly the behavior I wanted.

Concern: My dog will be out of control. Your dog will not be out of control just because you used positive methods. Using positive methods, like clicker training, doesn't mean that you are permissive with your dog. It is important to establish rules, boundaries, and consistency by *always* following through. For example, you have established the rule in your house, that no dogs are allowed on the couch. Your dog jumps up on the couch, and you tell him to get down. He looks at you with those puppy eyes, and how do you respond?

Do you follow through with the rule and walk over to him and help him down? Or do you respond by being permissive and allow him to snuggle up with you to watch a movie "just this once"? Do you allow your dog to pull on the leash to see someone "just this once"? Or do you follow through and make sure that he is walking on a loose leash to a person that he wants to see? *Consistency is a major element to successfully training and controlling your dog.* Using a clicker is merely a positive reinforcement tool.

The "How To" of the Marker Method
Once you have accepted the advantages of clicker training, it is important to next understand the steps in using marker training. I use the word *click* interchangeably with the word *mark*. The steps

below can be applied whether you use a word like "yep," whistle, snap your fingers, or use a clicker. For me personally, I have trained with a clicker as well as using the word "yep."

Loading the Marker

Before you actually begin with the clicker training, however, you will want to accustom your dog to the sound of the clicker by doing what trainers call "loading the clicker." This means that your dog will associate the sound of the click with something wonderful. What you do to load the clicker is click and deliver a treat. When he's finished chewing, you will click and deliver another treat. You will repeat this process several times, 6-10 clicks/6-10 treats. You will later go back and repeat the steps for loading the marker except that now you will use your verbal marker. For example, I will say "yep" and then deliver a treat, repeating 6-10 times.

Now it's time to put clicker training into action.

Michelle's Steps in Clicker Training

1. **Mark (click) the desired behavior.** During this step you choose *one* behavior to mark. For example, if you are working on a *sit*, then only click *sit*. Do not click a *down* or a *watch*. You must only click for a *sit*. Clicking other behaviors will lead to confusion. When your dog is easily and quickly offering you the

behavior you set out to establish every time, you are ready to move on to the next step.

How do you know you've established a behavior? You are in the kitchen cooking when you look at him, and he quickly goes into a "sit," which is what you taught him to do; you are outside pulling weeds, and when you look at him, he goes into a *sit*, which is what you taught him to do; or before you give him his food bowl, you look at him and he goes into a *sit*, which, again, is what you taught him to do. You know you have established the behavior that you want.

2. **Name the behavior.** You will still continue marking (clicking) as in step one, but you will also add the name of the behavior (*down, sit, come*, etc.). You can say the name of the behavior as he's in position. This, in my opinion, is a more difficult step for the dog because dogs don't easily learn verbal cues. You can, if desired, add non-verbal cues, like hand signals. It is your preference. I encourage my students to use verbal cues because when a guest walks into your house, what do they do? They start chanting "sit" to your dog. The person doesn't know you have a non-verbal hand signal, so teaching a verbal cue, especially for a behavior like *sit*, will help set your dog up for success regardless of who is issuing the cue.

Nonetheless, a dog's first language is body language. They are so gifted at watching all of our tiny movements, understanding our moods, knowing when we plan to leave the house, and so much more. More than likely, this adept sense plays a role in why it is difficult to train dogs to learn a verbal cue versus a hand signal. Many times dogs will see a micro movement in our body language and think that's the cue while all along we think they've successfully learned the verbal cue. For example, a friend once said to me, "Michelle, your son (referring to my dog, Boy) doesn't know how to sit." I replied, "What do you mean, my son doesn't know how to sit? He knows how to sit!" She responded, "Fine, stand up straight, put your hands behind your back, and say 'sit.' I did just that, but Boy continued to stand wagging his tail. But then I leaned slightly forward, and he went into a *sit* clearly in response to the slight change in my posture. It's important that we become aware of our own body language, and as the handlers, we go out of our way to ensure that our dog learns the verbal cue. If your dog has learned to sit only when you lean slightly forward, he will not respond to guests that say "sit" without the additional body language.

Teach English as a Second Language
Develop good training habits. For instance, when you see your dog move into a down position naturally on his own, say, "*Down*, good *down*." Praise him saying, "Good *sit*," or "Good *come*," instead of simply saying,

"Good boy!" Say the cue word as much as possible to help teach the dog your language.

When should you move on to step three? Be sure not to move on too quickly. Say the name with the behavior to gain the association as much as possible, even up to two weeks if necessary. The ultimate test is to say the cue and wait for the response. If your dog performs the behavior quickly, then he has an understanding of the word and you can move on to step three.

3. **Cue the behavior and wait for a response.** Once your dog understands the association of the cue with the behavior, you may continue with step three. For a week, cue the behavior and as soon as it is performed, click the behavior and reinforce with a treat or other reinforcement. During this step you will work on speed (how quickly the dog responds after hearing the cue). Eventually you can start delivering a "jackpot" of treats, several delivered one at a time, for quick responses.

4. **Add stimulus control to the cue.** The wonderful thing about clicker training is that dogs freely offer behaviors. The problem, however, is that if you don't get the cued behavior under stimulus control (only performed when asked), he will continue to offer the behavior in a buffet type style as an attempt to earn a click from you. How do you

achieve the desired response only when you want it? You will start to click and reward only when the behavior is performed after the verbal cue. To do this, train in specific formal sessions during step four. If your dog performs a behavior you didn't cue, wait 20-30 seconds and re-cue the behavior; then click for the right response. Once you've worked on stimulus control for several weeks, then you add the behavior to the repertoire of established cues, clicking only the right response to the behaviors you cue. Do not neglect this step! Otherwise, you may spend a lifetime of getting every trick in the book for the desired response.

But He's Scared of the Sound

If your dog is afraid of the sound of the clicker, you can use an I-click® which has a softer click, a pen/retractable pencil, or a verbal marker, "yes."

To teach a verbal marker like "yes," you will load the word "yes" just as explained earlier on loading the clicker. You will follow all four steps in training, but instead of clicking, you will mark with "yes" or "yep" as I do. You can use whatever verbal cue you would like. However, I would again caution you about using the word "good" or "good boy" as dogs hear those phrases from you all the time. You want the marker to be distinct for him to identify.

Above, pictured to the left are box clickers and to the right is an I-click®.

Environmentally Cued

The great thing about the clicker is that you are able to reinforce behaviors that you don't necessarily add a cue to. In other words, I can use the click to reinforce a behavior that I don't always want to name like *sit* or *down*, but just want to see more of. Specifically with *come*, I will reinforce the dog's behavior of checking in with me. So, when I am outside and I see his eyes move in my direction, I will click, allow him to move towards me, and then give him a reward. I am not necessarily cueing anything verbally but reinforcing the behavior of looking at me and moving toward me. This freedom from saying a cue is what I love about the clicker! We will use the clicker (or marker) from time to time throughout the exercises in this book.

CHAPTER 3
NOW YOU KNOW

The way that you respond to your dog's behavior creates an emotional response for him. Let's think about this for a minute. Let's say that you are in the beginning stages of falling in love with someone. Your emotions are strong. You have this yearning to be with that person. You can't wait to be with together. It's intense. There are butterflies, roses, and rainbows when you think of this person or hear this person's name. You are eager to spend time together.

On the other end of the spectrum, maybe you've been fighting with someone for months. Everything now that he/she says and does annoys you. You even hate the way he or she holds the fork, chews food, or says certain words. You cannot even stand the idea of being in the same room with that person.

Emotional associations matter for us, and emotions matter for dogs as well. Your response, positive or negative, to your dog coming to you will make all the difference in the world.

Has your dog ever run away from you? What did you do? If your dog does run away from you, never, ever,

ever (Did I say that enough times??) punish, yell, spank, or act annoyed with your dog. Please. *Never.* The way that you respond to your dog, especially with the cue *come*, will determine his response. It's important to appear unfazed even if you are upset. You want him to *want* to come to you, not the opposite.

But It's a Negative

For a moment let's think about things from the dog's perspective. You have a coworker that starts off saying something positive, but you know she will end with a negative. "You did a good job, BUT..." "I like your shirt, but gosh, it's probably too tight for the office." You will begin to dread any sort of positive thing that comes out of her mouth because you know that there is a negative "but" that follows.

Similarly, when working on the *come* cue, you must always think about things from the dog's perspective. In other words, what is negative for him? And whatever is negative for him, do not pair it with the cue *come*. What does this mean? A very good example would be illustrated in my group class for basic manners where we work on recalls. The dog comes running in hard to the owner and performs what is actually quite a beautiful *come*. When the dog gets close to the owner to get his yummy treat, the owner gives it to him and then starts petting him like crazy. Typically what I see at this point is the dog backing up. He is backing up because at that moment *he did not want to be petted.* He wanted a treat. Now, because of this first association, on the second recall that we do, the dog doesn't run as fast to the owner.

What are some things that your dog may perceive as a negative?

- When he is at the dog park, and owner cues *come*, leashes the dog and then leaves the park.
- Before leaving for work, owner cues *come,* and puts the dog in the kennel for 7 hours.
- Owner cues *come.* The dog runs up to the owner, and the owner pets the dog. The dog backs up because he doesn't enjoy someone petting his face.

A negative doesn't necessarily have to come in the form of you yelling at your dog. A negative is anything that he finds unpleasant or he just doesn't like. You want the cue *come* to mean rainbows and butterflies, a day without rain or flies, because feelings really do matter.

Hear the cue "come" → Feel happy → Run to owner

Eww, Yuck!
So one of the most rewarding things that I have going on in my life is being a mother. I have beautiful identical twin boys that rock my world. They will soon be 4 years old as I write this. Sometimes the things they say crack me up.

A few mornings ago I was making my green drink (yes, a health nut too). I mix carrot juice with my green drink. Anthony saw the carrot juice and wanted some. I poured a little bit into his cup and handed it to him. After he tasted it, I asked, "You like it, Anthony?" "No!" he said as he placed the cup back on the counter. "YUCK!" As a result of this negative experience, he won't even touch an orange-colored juice again. Why? Because the first orange-colored drink he tried was gross to him, and that was that.

There are times that the cue *come* has become like carrot juice to Anthony. He sees it, and he is not interested. Your dog hears *come* and he runs away from you. The scientific term for this is a "poisoned cue," a result that occurs from calling *come* and doing something your dog doesn't like (putting him into a kennel, leaving him for the day, petting him in a way he doesn't appreciate, or putting him into the tub for a bath, etc.), but it can also be caused by punishing your dog. Let's just say your dog runs away, and you finally catch him and then spank him. If I were your dog, I wouldn't ever want to come to you again either!

When I had my training facility in Iowa, I had a couple working with me on *come* with their dog. They said their dog knew *come*, so I had them say their recall cue and then watched their dog literally run as fast as he could to the opposite end of the facility. They obviously had poisoned the cue somewhere along the line.

If your cue has been poisoned, you will need to start from scratch. In other words, you will need to create a new *come* cue as if you have never taught *come* before. It is back to the basics for you and your dog.

Maybe It is What You Say
The sounds that we make communicate to dogs what we want. Horse trainers make a sound with the side of their mouth to encourage movement forward, and I make a similar sound with my dogs.

When I read Patricia McConnell's book *The Other End of the Leash*, I was fascinated with the research that she had conducted on sound for her doctoral study. Particularly fascinating to me was her discussion of the sounds trainers (no matter what language they spoke) made to get their horse or dog to stop, or move forward.

...Peruvian Quechua sheepdog handlers used short, repeated whistles and words to encourage their dogs to get moving. English-speaking sled dog racers belted out short, repeated sounds—words like 'Go! Go! Go!' and 'Hike! Hike! Hike!' and 'Hyah! Hyah!'—to encourage more speed from their dogs. In contrast, when handlers wanted to slow or stop an animal, they used one single, continuous note... Common English 'slow down' signals to dogs and horses are 'Stay,' 'whoa,' and 'easy'. [McConnell, Patricia, The Other End of the Leash 57]

So let's think about the cue that we use to get our

dogs to move towards us, the single word "come." Dr. McConnell's research suggests that using the word *come* in one short syllable will encourage a stop behavior versus a movement forward. This is why it's important that when you say *"come,"* you stretch out the word or sing their name before the cue *come* (change intonation of voice) as I do with my dogs.

Of Course How You Say It Matters

And, because it does matter, when I cue my dogs to come, I sing. I know, my students think I am nuts too. The thing, though, is that I am not complaining about their assessment of me because, guess what? Every time I call a dog, he comes. Why? Because I know how to use my tone of voice to encourage the dog's movement toward me.

When I sing, I hold out the *come* and use a high-pitched voice that I *only* use when I cue *come.*

As an illustration, I train many people's dogs at my house so there is a lot of traffic going in and out of my gates, and one afternoon I realized that someone hadn't latched the gate all of the way because my backyard was empty, and the front gate was swaying a bit in the wind. No dogs. Just like any other dog owner, I panicked. I said in a stern voice, "Dogs, come!" Nothing. Thoughts rushed through my head *Oh my gosh! My dogs have been trained! They know come! Why aren't they coming?! Oh my gosh! What if they get hit by a car?!* I snapped myself out of my state of panic and thought, *Duh, Michelle. Listen to how you cued come!* I sang my "Dogs, come!" and they all came bolting to me with grins on their faces.

The tone and the way that I sing the cue is also an effective tool to communicate to my dogs to speed up if they are going slower than I like or to slow down if they are going too fast. In my group classes we will say, "Puppy, puppy puppy" to help encourage speed with *come.* I encourage you, even if you can't bring yourself to sing, to find and employ some consistent means of issuing the cue.

Not Come Here, Come On; Just Come

As humans, we tend to be human, of course. I have realized with the help of friends and family that I am just as guilty of what I am about to talk about. For whatever reason, with the cue *come* especially, we tend to say it about 50 different ways. How confusing! Have you ever learned a second language? Often, languages offer a billion different ways to say the same thing. It is imperative when training for the dog who is learning English as his second language to be specific with a simple cue like *come.*

We all need to be aware of when we use this cue and how we use it! Otherwise, we are sending inaccurate signals and causing confusion.

Use Everyday Life to Your Advantage

There are many opportunities that life presents to us that we can easily create a positive association with the cue *come.*

- Cue *come,* and leash your dog to take him for a walk.

- Cue *come,* and give your dog a meal in his food bowl.
- Cue *come* when dogs are playing outdoors in a fenced-in yard, reward, and send them back out to play.
- Cue *come* as your dog is already on his way to you and reward with treats.
- If your dog enjoys car rides, cue *come* to get into car for a ride.

When Not to Say

If you know the situation is such that no matter how well your dog is trained, he *is not* going to *come,* do not call him. I had my "ah ha" moment with Boy when he was staring at a rabbit through the window, and I called "come." Epic fail. Be sure to reserve this powerful word for times that *you know for sure* you will get a response. Doing so will increase the likelihood for your dog to *come* in dangerous or distracting situations, like running into the street.

Who Knew? How You Stand Matters

The way that you stand will affect how a dog responds to you.

You don't want to discourage a *come* with your posture. Bending over or stretching your hands out toward your dog are both postures that will discourage a *come* because these postures can be seen as threatening to a dog.

On the other hand, often times, squatting down will encourage a *come.*

How Dogs Understand Movement

If I wanted you to move closer to me, I would take steps toward you, and you would naturally take steps toward me. Dogs are the opposite. If I take two steps toward a dog, he will take two steps back. Have you ever noticed when you start to walk toward your dog, unlike a human, he will back up?

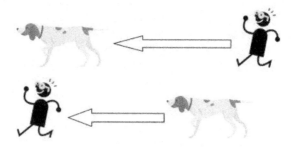

Use movement to Your Advantage

Use your body movement to encourage the *come*. In order to communicate *come* in a way that your dog will understand, you must use your whole body movement in the opposite direction that you want him to move.

Understanding these basic premises about dogs' perceptions will put you well on your way to achieving a symbiotic relationship with your pet so that he will want to come to you each and every time.

CHAPTER 4
REINFORCEMENT

"The most important fact to remember is that dog training is constantly going on whether or not people are actually involved in it."Bruce Fogle [The Dog's Mind 98]

Reinforcement is your key to your ultimate desire of getting your dog to come every time. If you learn how to use this tool with skill, you will be extremely successful.

"Dogs don't need teachers to condition their minds. They don't even have to be in a 'learning' frame of mind. Our role in operant learning, in dog training, is technically speaking, not to be the 'teacher' but to be the 'controller.' Dogs are learning all the time and our objective is to control the stimuli, responses and rewards. We can do so by reinforcing..." Bruce Fogle [The Dog's Mind 99]

Reinforcement applied in exercise, such as lifting weights, causes our muscles to become stronger. Reinforcement is equally as important when applied in the training program with your dog.

Reinforcement is *the act of strengthening or encouraging something; a thing that strengthens or encourages something* (Online Merriam-Webster)

What can be used as a reinforcement in training? Anything that your dog sees as desirable. Reinforcement, for you too, is something that you see as desirable. As humans, we all work for money. Money is a huge motivator, and we will do some great things for the sake of it. Money to a dog smells interesting, but I doubt that you could get more than three sits for a hundred dollar bill.

Aside from money, motivators can come in many different forms for humans. The environment and temperature can also be appealing reinforcements for us, depending on the time of year. Because they make us feel good, we gravitate toward the fan or fireplace.

When I am training a dog, I will use many reinforcers aside from food such as allowing him to chase a blowing leaf along the road or smell a tree or post or, perhaps, play a game of tug.

Reinforcement is always changing
And because it is, you must be willing to reevaluate what will motivate your dog under the circumstances at that moment. I find this statement true, especially when training in the outdoors. One minute my dog desires a cooked hotdog, and the next minute he wants to sniff the mailbox post. Competing for

attention when training in an environment so rich to a dog can be viewed as a struggle, or you can look at it as an opportunity to be observant and to change your reinforcement to what your dog desires in that moment.

For example, your dog is pulling you because there is a specific patch of grass he would like to go sniff. We can either see that patch of grass as frustrating, or we can see it as an opportunity. Now is the time to think, *"Aha, puppy dog, you really want to go sniff those blades of grass, a beautiful opportunity. But, first, puppy, we must get there on a loose leash."*

Reinforcement is always chosen by the learner I just mentioned a moment ago that I really doubt that you could get your dog to do more than three sits by rewarding with a hundred dollar bill. Though your dog might be unwilling to sit for a hundred bucks, he might be more than willing to sit for something far simpler and less expensive. Whoever you are teaching or training is the one that gets to choose what's worth his time.

Other Examples of Reinforcers:

Sniffing an area of grass
Chasing a leaf being blown in the wind
Going to another dog
Safely chasing a bird
A game that he enjoys

Timing matters

When you deliver treats or any other reinforcement, the timing is important. Imagine these two scenarios:

Show Treat → Call "come" → Dog comes → Deliver treat

Call "come"→ Dog comes → Deliver treat

Do you see the difference? It's important that you get the behavior first before delivering the reinforcement or even allowing him to see the treat. Why? Because in the first situation you are offering him a bribe. What will end up happening with the first scenario, which is a frequent complaint that I hear from dog owners when they come the first night of class, is, "My dog will only lie down for a treat." Or another classic one is that the dog only comes when he hears the owner shaking the bag of treats. These techniques are not good training methods nor will they give you the strong desired behaviors that I know you want. If you train using the treat first before the cue or behavior, you will always be stuck doing so. With good training skills, a handler will wait for the desired behavior and then deliver the treat.

"The timing, intensity and intervals of reinforcement all have direct consequences on learned behaviour. Reinforcement must be immediate. Giving a dog a reward at the end of training is pointless because you're not reinforcing behaviour immediately. To the

dog's mind, a reward must be instantaneous if the behaviour is to be reinforced. " Bruce Fogle *[The Dog's Mind 100]*

Don't Be Stingy

The number of treats (or length of time reinforcement is given) matters. In other words, if I have been working toward a specific behavior in a training session, and my dog finally performs that behavior, I will deliver a jackpot. A jackpot is several treats delivered one at a time, one right after the other. Just as for a person winning a jackpot of money on a slot machine, the method is a key to strengthening the dog's behavior for the next time. The big win keeps the human playing the slot machine because of the hope of a big pay off just as the dog will continue to work toward his big pay off in the form of a jackpot of treats.

On the other hand, this doesn't mean that you should deliver three treats at once every time you are reinforcing a behavior. Your dog will get fat this way. However, for the moments that you see the behaviors that are fantastic because they looked exactly how you wanted them to look, or your dog has been working hard in a session and he finally achieves the desired behavior, it's time to give a jackpot.

"The schedule of the reinforcement of behaviour is also important in modifying the dog's mind..... Continuous reinforcement by which a behaviour is rewarded each time leads to rapid learning." Bruce Fogle [The Dog's Mind 100]

Remember though, a jackpot doesn't always have to come in the form of food. I was working with a student's dog on gaining focus while leashed. After I had gotten the dog to walk several steps alongside me with a *watch* cue, I released the dog, and we played a 1-minute game of tug, an activity I knew the dog immensely enjoyed and would find as satisfying as several treats. When we returned to leash walking, the dog was even more engaged. Being skilled in reinforcement is a huge part of a successful training program.

Change Your Perspective of Treats

Dogs can work because of respect or love for us, but they also need a stronger motivation. Treats or food are a paycheck to a dog. As long as treats are used in the correct order and manner as previously described, then your dog is simply getting paid for doing his "job."

Get the behavior you want→ Deliver the treat

Be outrageously generous with rewards. Training the recall is no time to be stingy! Use meat-based treats, a large portion of your dog's daily kibble, a game of tug – anything your dog loves. Never show her the food or toy before you call her, though. Use these as rewards after correct behavior, not as bribes to encourage it. If your dog can predict what reward you have up your sleeve, she can also calculate when it's in her best interest to ignore your recall cue. So make a point of being variable with your rewards. – Kathy Sdao [www.kathysdao.com]

Think of Treats as Money

As you are working toward a desired behavior (like eye contact, *come*, etc.), you will want to reinforce. Begin to view your treats, praise, or other reinforcers as money. Each time you deliver a treat, there is a coin going into your piggy bank of behavior. Before you know it, you have a pretty strong "bank of behavior" account.

What It Will Become

Obviously, as you work through the training process and behaviors become well established, you will not use the same amount of treats as you once did, but you will still randomly reinforce. As I mentioned previously, I am currently potty training two three-year old boys. Let's just say this is not easy! Any time they go on the potty, they earn a sticker. For whatever reason, flushing the toilet seems to serve as a reinforcement to them as well. It would seem pretty ridiculous to reinforce them when they are 10 for going potty. They will have learned the skill, and the behavior is established.

What are "Go to" Reinforcers?

Again, during the process of training, *reinforcement is always chosen by the dog,* and the *reinforcement is always changing.* Within a three-minute training session, I may reward three pieces of chicken and a release to go sniff a mailbox. It all depends on what I notice my dog is interested in at the moment.

It's important to watch your dog to see what he wants at *a particular moment,* use that desire to get what you want, and then give him what he wants. This idea is called the Premack Principle.

With the following types of reinforcers, you will release your dog with a *go* cue. For example, I see my dog really wants to go sniff a specific area of grass, but he's starting to pull. Great! Though I am not thrilled that he is pulling, here is an excellent opportunity for training!

The idea of giving in to something that seems "naughty," like allowing my dog to chase a squirrel, almost seems backwards, but it works, and it is a good example of the Premack Principle in practice. One of my favorite trainers Kathy Sdao was sharing with us during a seminar about training dolphins. Kathy worked as a contractor with the military. She trained wild dolphins to detect mines in the ocean. There is a specific time of year when the whales would migrate in, and the dolphins loved to play on the waves these whales made. Kathy used the Premack Principle (Remember, you get what you want, and then give your dog what he wants). The dolphins that she was working with were wild and free, but even so, Kathy would get a behavior that she wanted from the dolphin and release the dolphin to go play.

This same principle can be used with the dreaded squirrel. Obviously, first making sure that both dog and squirrel are safe, you can "chase" a squirrel with a dog. When I've done this with dogs, we chase a couple feet, and usually within a few seconds, the squirrel is headed up a tree. This principle works.

I love implementing the Premack Principle because we can allow our dogs to pursue all of the so-called "naughty" behaviors that we tend to fight. The trick is to use those "naughty" behaviors to your advantage. It's like finally giving in to the current of the river and just going with the flow. Nature is always going to win, so you might as well go with it and make it work for you.

Reinforcement Makes Behavior Stronger
Reinforcement is the key to every behavior you want. Be a student of your dog and begin to look for things

that he really enjoys, and use those things to your advantage.

Just as you focus on things your dog likes, you should also consider things that you do that he doesn't like.

For example, I will see a dog perform an excellent behavior like ringing the bell to go potty, and as I am observing my student work with the dog, who is waiting for him/her to throw chicken on the floor, the student starts petting the dog. I see the dog backing up, clearly not thrilled about the owner's notion of reinforcement.

Over all the years of training, I have only worked with one dog who enjoyed being petted more than receiving food or other reinforcers; that's how rare it is.

I have heard this principle articulated in the perspective of working hard on a project at work, expecting a raise. After the project is complete, your boss stops in and tells you what a fabulous job you've done, and your reward is going out to supper with him and his wife for the evening. Thud!

So, besides being a student of your dog to see what he likes, be aware of how human you are and that there may be things that you are doing that are only a reinforcement in your own perception.

Follow Through

If you are a parent or have observed parents, you are aware that following through with what you say is extremely important. If I am at a restaurant with my twin boys and tell them to sit down in their chair more than once, I will "help" them sit down.

Dogs are like kids in that they need consistency. Even as adults we need consistency. We need to know the exact tasks our employer expects us to accomplish by a specific deadline. We would not appreciate our employer changing the deadline from day to day. Likewise, dogs want to know what is expected of them and when it is expected, and they thrive when the follow-through is consistent.

Be Consistent After Saying Your Cue

For instance, if you cue "*sit*" in a location when you feel your dog can successfully focus, but he doesn't sit, you need to be consistent and follow through. There are times when my dog Boy decides he doesn't want to get down from the couch. If I know with certainty that he heard my cue but didn't move, I will walk toward the couch to follow through, and within seconds he will jump down. When your dog does not respond to your cue, you get out of your chair, so to speak, and encourage the dog to follow through. Remember, unlike humans, dogs are not verbal; they read body language. You must use your body's movement at times to follow through.

MICHELLE HUNTTING

CHAPTER 5
ATTENTION!

I was involved in the military community for over nine years. It is still pretty amazing to me that when "attention" is cued to the soldiers, they all squirm quickly to get into place and make themselves stiffer than an ironing board. The military trained this response. If I talked to soldiers to inquire about their emotional response to this cue, I would guess that it may not have a positive emotional response, but, nonetheless, it is one that evokes quick movement.

Eye Contact   Leave it!   Movement toward you

We want to create a positive emotional response to your dog when he hears his name. We want his name to become an "attention" cue so that he will immediately search and look for you when he hears it.

What's in a Name? Say "No" to No

There are times when pet owners frequently use the word "no" with their dog. I have found this to be problematic because more often than not, the puppy or dog will begin to associate *no* as his name. Please be aware of this potentiality and avoid overusing *no*.

"Penny, Penny, Penny"

One of my favorite shows over the years is *The Big Bang Theory*. If you have ever watched the show, you know Sheldon always repeats Penny's name to the point of ridiculous and unnecessary. As humans, we have been conditioned to respond to our names. We don't always act right away because we may be in the middle of a thought, walking to answer the door, finishing up one thing before going to the next, but we for sure heard our name, and it evoked a response. As long as you have conditioned your dog to his name (exercises mentioned later in this chapter), then he heard you, and I, from observation, can tell that he had a response. There is no need to say his name or the cue over and over again.

If you have engaged in this unfortunate behavior, then you have conditioned your dog with a new cue. Let's say, for example, your cue is "Penny, come." Perhaps your dog doesn't look at you in the first nanosecond, so you say, "Penny! Penny! Penny!" After several repetitions your cue has now become "Penny! Penny! Penny! Come!"

Be aware of your urge to repeat as you work with your dog. No chanting allowed! If you have been chanting, then I would suggest starting over from scratch with a new cue.

Because *come* is *the most important cue* to provide for your dog's safety, it is important that your cue be short and concise. A situation might someday arise where you do not have time to chant your dog's name before receiving a response.

Consider this possibility: Imagine that he is in the middle of the road sniffing a spot and you yell his name, but because he has become accustomed to hearing it in repetition, he continues sniffing. A car is approaching.... You get the point.

It's All About the Eyes
One of the key foundational skills with *come* is eye contact between the pet and owner. I have included exercises below that will aid you in this process. From here on out, any eye contact needs to be recognized whether you are in a training session or not. We need to make eye contact worth his time because you will be competing with the world and its rich environment.

Let's say just for a moment that I want to encourage you to look at me. When we are inside the house, every single time you look at me, I will reinforce your eye contact by handing you a combination of $1, $5, or $10 bills. Looking at me now has not only become fun, but you will continue to do it because your piggy bank is growing. Then, when we go outside, every single time you look at me I will hand you $25, $50, or $100. You will more than likely continue so that you earn the reward.

For a dog, money is just a shred of paper and not all that exciting, but beef liver or some other crazy smelling meat is. Think about what you use to reinforce him in these terms when it comes to eye contact, one of the three pillars of a strong recall. Once again, note that it all goes back to what will make it worth *his* while to perform the behavior.

The Name Game
Training your dog to respond to his name should be done indoors until his response becomes fluent. When it is, you can move outdoors to the backyard, front yard, park, and so forth.

> Tip: When outdoors, keeping your dog on a dropped leash is helpful so that you can use it if it becomes necessary to get his attention.

Allow your dog to get distracted with sniffing some objects.

When he is distracted, say his name one time. Watch

his neck. As soon as you see his neck start turning towards you, mark and treat.

Caution: Allow the dog to come to you. Do not walk towards your dog to hand him the treat. You will repeat this exercise five times and end the session. You can perform this exercise once a day.

If your dog doesn't turn his head after you have waited three seconds, you will "move in on the leash." Have you ever choked up on the bat? You move your hands up farther toward the barrel.

Similarly, you will pick up his leash and "choke up," moving toward him gradually, watching for his neck to turn. Once he does, mark and treat. However, unless he looks at you beforehand, when your hands move up the leash to the point where they are six inches away from his neck, bend your face down. He now has fewer options. One, he can look at you, or two, he can look away. As soon as he turns toward you, click and treat.

Watch Exercise

Another simple daily exercise that you can do is to take a handful of treats out to the front yard. Make a fist around the treats and place behind your back. With your other hand, hold one treat in front of his nose and draw the treat up to your face next to your eyes. As soon as you get the treat up to your eyes, quickly say your marker and deliver the treat. Repeat until all treats are gone. As you progress with this exercise, you can delay saying your marker word as you work on the duration of eye contact.

Hanging Out in the Park

Every couple of weeks, go to a park with your dog and take along a blanket that you can both sit on. Take along something to read so that your dog is unaware that a training exercise is involved, and be sure to take a stuffed Kong® or some sort of chewy that your dog can enjoy. Watch your dog's eyes. Every time your dog looks at you, click and give a *high*-value treat.

Caution: As a reminder, bait bags often cue a dog that it is time to train, and they may become conditioned to listen only when they see the bait bag. Use it sparingly, and mix it up by stowing the treats in other locations such as pockets.

CHAPTER 6
LEAVE IT!

If you think about it, when you call "come," in order for the dog to comply, the dog must leave whatever he's interested in, look for you, and then move toward you. There are three important steps in complying with *come.* Each step takes much impulse control, so working on each skill separately until they are fluid is very important. *Leave it!* is pillar two in a solid recall.

Eye Contact Leave it! Movement toward you

Leave It!
A solid *leave it!* cue will not only promote impulse control and focus but will also be instrumental in eliciting a solid *come.* Obviously, the *leave it!* cue could save your dog's life in the event you drop a pill on the floor. (Pills for humans can pose grave danger

to our canine companions.) Or, if your dog is curious like Boy was about peanut butter on Grandpa's mouse trap, a strong response to the *leave it! cue could save your dog's snout!* Establishing this cue with a high skill level is crucial for *come.* Your dog is not going to leave something that is very intriguing unless you've taught him that you have something more worth his while and also help him establish the necessary impulse control skills.

Proper command of the *leave it!* cue will progress to the point where you can throw hotdogs at your dog's face, and he will leave them alone. How can the dog have such amazing control? You have taught him that if he leaves it as you have cued, he will get something even better. For example, if I asked you to drop a $50 bill, "No way, Miss Michelle." But if I said, "If you drop that $50 bill, I'll give you a $100 bill," then you would willingly relinquish it.

You never know when you will need to use the *leave it!* cue. When I first moved back to North Carolina in 2009, I was taking my three dogs for a walk. I knew that Morgan had picked up something in her mouth, but honestly, I wasn't sure what it was. I cued "leave it," and to my disbelief, Morgan proceeded to spit an entire six-inch Subway® sandwich out of her mouth and then proudly looked at me. To this day, I am still amazed that Morgan listened to me because the sandwich was such a high value item to her. Training pays off. You never know what your dog might find, might get into, or what strangers may offer him. Teaching *leave it!* is a safety cue in addition to helping with impulse control and focus. It's a must tool to have with *come.*

How to Teach "Leave it!":
When teaching the cue *leave it!*, you will need to use treats that are of equal or lesser value to your dog.

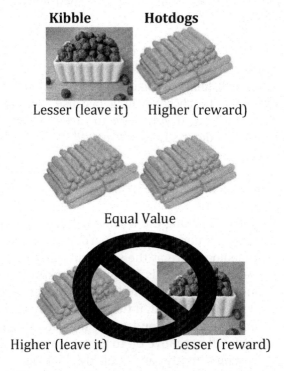

Kibble   **Hotdogs**

Lesser (leave it)   Higher (reward)

Equal Value

Higher (leave it)   Lesser (reward)

You will ask your dog to leave a lower level treat and reward with a higher level treat. A higher level treat for my dogs would be a hotdog, and a lower level treat would be a piece of their dog food. Every dog will vary in preference just as humans have varied preferences. Some of us would enjoy chicken over steak, for example. The point is that you are asking your dog to leave the $50 and rewarding with a $100 bill.

Tip: Never release your dog to go get the treat or item you just told him to leave. The reason for this is that in a non-training situation you would never release him to get something you cued *leave it!* Be consistent.

In addition, the *leave it!* cue is always cued first unlike other taught cues. The reason for this is that your dog will know immediately if you don't want him to get or touch something because you always say "leave it!" But if you were to throw a ball or a treat, and you don't say the "*leave it!*" cue, he knows he is free to go for it!

Steps for teaching "leave it!":

1. Show your dog the treat. Cue "leave it!" Place the treat under your shoe. Your dog can dig at the shoe, stare at the shoe, but what you will be watching for is for him to look up at you, look away from the hidden treat, or best of all, back away from it. If the dog does any of these behaviors, click and treat. Repeat the game. You will not move on to the next step until he is consistently and quickly looking away, looking at you, or backing up when you cue "leave it!"

Michelle is cueing Boy to "leave it!"

2. This time, place a treat beside your shoe, but be ready to cover the treat quickly with your shoe if he goes for it. You will be watching for him to look up at you, look away, or, again, hopefully back away. When he does any of these actions, click and treat. Repeat the game. As in step 1, you will not move on to the next step until he is consistently and quickly looking away, looking at you, or backing up when you cue "leave it!"

Michelle is placing treat beside her shoe.

Boy looked at Michelle's face, so Michelle clicked and rewarded.

As you work through steps 2-18, you will progress in your dog's skill level with *leave it*! With each step you will continue to click and treat when he looks away, looks at you, or backs away.

3. Start dropping the treat from a higher level.

Note: If you have a petite breed or a dog with less vigor, then using your hand rather than your shoe to cover up the treat is totally acceptable. I have included pictures demonstrating using a fist/hand for the first process of teaching *leave it!* In the past five years I have started using my shoe because, with the larger dogs I train, my hand had been "dug at" with paws way too many times.

Michelle is making a fist around the treat.

Make a fist and push against the ground with your fist.
In this picture Boy looked away after hearing the
"leave it!" cue, so Michelle clicked and rewarded him.

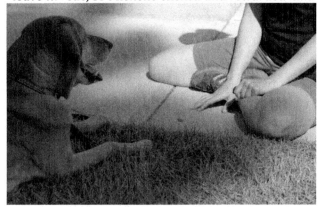

The next step is to leave the treat uncovered.

On the remaining steps, you will not proceed until your dog is consistent and quick to respond. Again what you will be watching for is for him to look away, look at you, or back away.

4. Start by dropping several treats from one inch off the ground.

5. Drop one treat from a higher distance.
6. Drop several treats from a higher distance.
7. Start by throwing one treat beside the dog. (Be sure you can cover it up if he goes for the treat.)

8. Throw one treat toward the dog.
9. Throw one treat beside the dog.
10. Throw several treats beside the dog.

11. Throw one treat toward the dog.
12. Throw several treats toward the dog.

13. Place a treat on the dog's paw while working toward placing several.
14. Start varying your position. If you were sitting, stand now and start at the beginning steps.
15. Take this activity to new locations, but be sure to start at the beginning steps and work up.
16. Now start introducing the cue *leave it!* Cue with neutral objects. (Remember, neutral objects such as a pencil would elicit no emotional response from your dog.)
17. Now use the cue *leave it!* with more desired objects. After your dog is doing well in a formal session, you can cue "leave it!" with objects that you plant for him to find in the house or yard. Be sure to reward with equal or higher value. For example, when I ask my dog to leave his Loofa® stuffed dog, I will reward with his tennis ball and a game of

fetch, the combination of which he values more than the stuffed dog.

18. Start using *leave it!* with people that the dog knows. Allow your dog to go up to this person and cue "leave it!"

Clearly, teaching the *come* cue requires foundational skills that exceed that one simple command. Investing the time into rewarding, reinforcing, and teaching the *leave it!* cue will be well worth your investment in time and energy. There is simply no substitute for a well-trained, safe dog.

Impulse Control

I just recently talked to a student of mine concerning her dog's ability with *come.* She has an adolescent dog and complained to me that he was doing great during formal training sessions, but when certain events interfered, he struggled and many times failed to recall.

Just as with any behavior that we train, it's important to keep in mind your dog's ability. Various factors, including the following, may affect your dog's ability to achieve a successful *come*: his age, the particular item that you are trying to pull him away from, the environment at that moment, and how much you've trained prior, just to name a few.

With my students and others in the training world, I am probably most recognized for my focus and emphasis on impulse control. In my opinion, many dogs are often willing to comply with a training skill during a formal training session, but when everyday "life happens," the dog may not have the impulse control skills to even think through his "arousal." At that point he is unable to comply with anything that he has been trained. It's not because he is being disobedient; *he is physically unable to comply*. Such is occasionally the case with my toddlers when they get so angry about something they are denied that, instead of taking a deep breath and gaining control of their emotions, they simply throw themselves down on the floor in a tantrum. Their impulse control skills at age three are not developed. It's my duty as a parent to guide them through the process of learning these skills and teach them how to properly handle themselves regardless of the circumstances. As pet parents, we have the same duty to help our dogs learn impulse control skills.

In my book *Control on Leash,* I write about my research on biofeedback in which the dog learns how to use his own body to calm himself down. I suggest numerous exercises to teach dogs impulse control. If you find that your dog is still struggling a lot with recalls after you have presented the techniques for *come* in this book, my strongest suggestion would be to consider the biofeedback exercises in *Control on Leash* and incorporate them into your training regimen. The result should be a solid recall even when your dog is faced with extreme distractions that he would otherwise not be able to pull himself away from.

In the case of my student with the adolescent dog, his age alone was an obstacle within himself that prevented him from consistently achieving a recall. However, with the introduction of some biofeedback skills, we were able to reach a much greater level of success. I am confident that his success level will continue to increase as he matures.

CHAPTER 7
COME GAMES

Moving Toward You

The behavior of moving toward you is pillar three of a strong recall. After training for several years, I have found these exercises to be some of my favorites. I know that you will enjoy these with your dog.

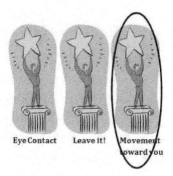

Eye Contact   Leave it!   Movement toward you

Note: Many, if not most, new handlers will get a great recall, and when the dog is close, the handler will cue a *sit*. When you are working on *come*, what is our one criterion? For the dog to come in close enough that we can touch his collar. Be happy right now with a fast recall. Adding a *sit* with the *come* can be done later. (Personally, I do not require these two together

61

from my dogs.)

Also when delivering the treat, be sure to avoid extending the treat toward your dog. Remember, you want to present the reward *after* the behavior is complete.

The Leash

Dogs become accustomed to the feeling of the leash and are very aware of when you take the leash off. Many dogs, when they hear the clip of the leash or don't feel the pressure of the leash, will run away from the owner. Sometimes the owner unknowingly causes this behavior by reinforcing it. For example, the owner may unclip the dog at the dog park and say excitedly, "Okay! Go play!" By showing excitement, the owner is inadvertently reinforcing the undesired behavior of running when the leash is unclipped.

Instead of generating excitement, we want to create

"a no-big-deal" response when the leash is on or off. We also want to reinforce focus when the leash is off.

Leash Awareness:

- When working on *come,* hold the leash and often drop it, picking it up nonchalantly.
- Unclip the leash, and as soon as you do, drop a pile of treats and start walking away. As soon as your dog engages with you (gives you eye contact or follows you), click and reinforce with a jackpot.
- Allow your long line to drag when you work on some exercises to help him to generalize *come* whether he feels the leash on or off.
- When your dog is in a safe place, work off leash as this will help him respond to *come* whether he is on or off leash.

Using the Clicker for *Come*

If you plan to use the clicker for the *come* exercises, you will mark when your dog turns to look at you. So, for example, you say, "Boy!" When he looks, you will mark and then as he's moving toward you, call "come."

Check Ins

If you notice that your dog is already on his way to you, go ahead and add the cue, "*Dog's name, come!*" You can add the cue if your dog, on his own initiative, comes quickly inside or if you see him walking to you from the kitchen to the living room. The more you are able to say the cue when your dog *comes* to you and you reinforce the behavior with something amazing, the stronger your cue will become.

Few Steps Back

Take a handful of treats. With your dog on leash, allow him to get distracted. After he's busy sniffing something or engaged in something else, say his name. When he turns to look at you, click, take three to four steps backward, and then deliver yummy treats. Repeat until all treats are gone.

Ping Pong Puppy

Ping Pong Puppy is similar to the egg toss game, an "oldy goldy" game that we played every 4th of July when I was a kid in Iowa. You and a partner face each other in close proximity. Each takes a turn tossing the egg. Once the egg is successfully passed, then each person takes a step back to repeat. The goal of the game is to be the last pair without a broken egg. We are going to play this game with your dog, but instead of tossing an egg, we will call your dog to "come."

Two people stand six feet apart from each other with the dog in the middle. Each person takes a turn to call the dog, "Name, *come!*" Click as soon as he looks at you and treat when he gets to you. After each person has called him, take one step back. If your dog doesn't understand, then decrease the distance, and be sure to make the sessions short initially.

Continue adding more distance if your dog is successfully coming every time. As your dog is successful in the exercise, add more distractions. Head outdoors and try it with the lead on, of course. The lead is not for pulling; it's there in case your pup decides that the rabbit would be more fun than the hotdog treat. You do not want to get into the habit of relying on a leash to get your dog to come. If you do, you will be forever using the leash for recalls. I want you to have success with *come* whether your dog is on or off the leash.

Example of Ping Pong Puppy

Hide and Seek

Another fun game you can play in the house is Hide and Seek. Each person in the house needs treats. Everyone hides around in the house and takes turns calling the dog to *come*. "*Name, come!*" When he *comes*, deliver a few treats. The next person calls out, "*Name, come!*" Continue to re-hide. The kids really enjoy this activity, and the dog learns from the interaction.

Two-Person Game

The purpose of the "Two-Person Game" exercise is to help build a speedy response to *come* from your dog.

One person will hold the dog on leash. The other person (runner) will have a handful of treats. The runner will make a fist around the handful of treats and place his fist directly in front of the dog's nose, allowing the dog to sniff. The runner then takes off running across the yard, saying something very excited like, "Puppy, puppy, puppy." The runner will not say "*come*" or the dog's name at this time. When the runner gets to the designated point of the yard, he squats and says, "*Dog's name, come.*" The person holding the leash lets go. The dog runs to the runner, and the runner then starts delivering each treat one at a time. With each treat delivery, give praise. "That was such a good *come!*" "You are so awesome!" "Great job, Scruffy!"

Tip: It's important to set your dog up for success with the appropriate amount of distance. In other words, if your dog doesn't get to you quickly and immediately, then decrease the distance that you run.

One-Person Game

The same game above can be played with one person but will start with a pile of treats placed on the ground to distract the dog while the runner starts running. When the dog leaves or finishes the treats and runs to the runner, the runner will praise and treat three times, place another pile of treats on the ground, and repeat the game.

Hamburger, Yum

This is a great exercise to do in the backyard, on a trail that you walk your dog without leash, or in an open forest. You can prepare hamburger patties before a training session by cutting them into fourths. Before your dog is in the area that you would like to train, hide the hamburger up in trees or tall bushes, and mark with chalk so you know where you hid the hamburger. Then, take your dog on a walk in the area. As you come across the places with the hidden treasures, call "come" and reward with the hamburger that, from the dog's point of view, "falls from the sky."

Collar Grab

In a separate session from *come* games, start working on getting your dog used to having his collar grabbed. This is important because many times when dogs run away, you may get them semi close and reach for the collar, but the dog jumps back and starts playing a game. We want to avoid this behavior. As you do each exercise below, you can either treat as you are doing it (recommended if the dog is new to this exercise or uncomfortable) or after you do the exercise (recommended as you progress with exercise).

- Touch collar with one hand
- Touch the collar with both hands
- Move the collar with hand
- Move the collar with both hands
- Reach from one side and then opposite side
- Reach from top and then bottom

- Do these exercises from different angles standing up, sitting down, and leaning over your dog

Be sure as you work through this exercise that you are going slowly and paying attention to your dog's body language. If he seems uncomfortable, slow down. (Please see Chapter 13 for information on dog body language.)

Note: I do not recommend using the clicker for this exercise as both hands will be close to the dog's head and thus his ears. The clicker is very loud, and you don't want to cause any pain with the sound.

As You Progress in Training
After you have worked on the collar exercises for two weeks, begin to add it to the *come* exercise. Cue "come." As your dog looks toward you, mark, say "come," and as he advances toward you, deliver the

treat, simultaneously grabbing his collar. *From here on out, get in the habit of doing so.* Be sure to watch your dog's body language, and if he is acting uncomfortable with the collar grab, go back to doing the exercises separately. We do not want to poison the *come* cue.

MICHELLE HUNTTING

CHAPTER 8
PREPPING FOR LIFE

I know you will strive to set your dog up for success, but sometimes life just happens such as the kids leaving the door open, allowing the dog to run out. If your dog doesn't *come* when called, as I said before, do not repeat his name or the *come* cue. However, obviously in an emergency situation you will want to do what you need to do to get your dog to safety. Sometimes that may involve getting into your car and going to get your dog so he'll jump right in.

Remember that dogs understand movement differently than humans. We understand that if someone is walking toward us that they desire to get closer perhaps to engage in a conversation. For dogs, however, advancing toward them is a different story. Dogs move in the direction that they want you to go. For example, when dogs are herding sheep, they move into the sheep to get them to move forward. Does that make sense? For this reason, when a dog runs away, and the owner chases the dog, the dog runs farther away. The key is to move in the same direction that you want the dog to go as this will encourage your dog to follow you.

Other Ideas:

If your dog should happen to "escape," and as a pair you have not yet mastered the *come* command, following are some ideas you may wish to try in an emergency situation:

- Make a "party over here!" For example, start playing with something in the grass while talking excitedly about it. Usually the dog will come running out of curiosity.
- Tap your legs or clap.
- Squat down on the ground.
- Say "up, up, up, up" as you move away.

Now What?

After your dog finally gets back to you, do not yell at him. Instead, be calm. Take a deep breath, try to remain emotionless, and assess what happened. Once your dog is in a safe place, ask yourself:

- Are there management precautions that I need to set in place? Why was my dog able to bolt out of the door? If you find the "fault" to be yours, it's important for you to set your dog up for success by putting management techniques into place while you are training a strong recall. Be sure in your formal sessions to conduct training sessions in the doorway that he tends to bolt from. In the meantime, have a baby gate set up in the door to prevent any bolting. (Because I am a mom of twins, I am practically an expert on baby gates. If you are placing one in a high traffic area, I suggest using the gates with the door built in so the gate's presence won't be too much of an inconvenience for you or your family.)

- Did I ask too much of my dog not to expect that he would run out while I was standing with the door propped open talking to the delivery person?
- How can I avoid having my dog escape next time I'm talking to the delivery person?
- When I am working on a formal session, is there a specific skill that I need to focus on to avoid his running from the doorway again? (for example, working on *come* from the car)
- Could I have used my tone of voice or body position differently to help my dog in this situation?

Prevent Bolting

Generally speaking, bolting occurs for pet owners from a doorway, car, or when the leash is unclipped. Leash awareness is addressed in Chapter 7, but, for your dog's safety, I would specifically like to address the doorway and car risks.

The Doorway

Because dogs do not generalize easily, it's important to do the *come* exercises from Chapter 7 in the area from which your dog is bolting. Things to focus on in this particular area besides the *come* exercises are a strong *stay* and *go to mat*.

Go to Mat

Teaching *go to mat* is a shaping exercise. What does this mean? This means that we will take a complex behavior and break it down into small behaviors (cue "mat", dog runs to mat, goes into a *down*, and *stays* until released). We then build those behaviors and add all of them together.

Think of shaping your dog's behaviors like clay in the potter's hand. He starts with a lump and has the task of really forming the clay into something complex and beautiful. What you will be doing with your dog is similar in that you begin with something in large proportion and transform it into a fine movement, involving multiple skills. It's important to be patient during the process.

Shaping is different from luring. It is tempting to lure during the process of shaping (such as throwing a treat on the mat before the dog decides to go to the mat). Don't take any shortcuts in this process because the shortcuts will only slow you down in the long run. It's important that your dog decides to go to the mat on his own. Please do not lure!

How Do I Shape Go to Mat?

This exercise teaches your dog to go to a specific location on cue and remain there until you verbally release him. This behavior is also a targeting behavior.

When I train others the "*go to mat*" cue, I always give my students two ways to accomplish it: formal and the lazy man's way. I tend to mix the two versions together. Which approach you choose will depend upon your dog's training drive, attention span, and his level of understanding the clicker.

What will the end result look like? You will cue "mat," or whatever you want to name your verbal cue. Your dog will find his mat, run to it, go into a *down*, and wait to be released.

How to Teach

1. Pick up your mat and act as if it is the neatest thing in the whole world; then throw the mat down on the floor. You will use curiosity to your advantage. If he looks (even with a flick of the eye), walks toward the mat, sniffs it, puts a paw on it, you will click and treat these behaviors. Once he finishes his treat, you will pick up the mat and repeat. Be sure you always put the treats on the mat as opposed to handing him the treat, so he learns that it is a magical mat that produces wonderful things.

2. Continue clicking as your dog is interacting with the mat and placing treats on the mat. Do NOT add the cue at this point because the behavior doesn't look exactly as you want it to look. If your dog *sits* on the mat, give a jackpot, several treats delivered one at time, one right after each other. If he goes into a *down*, give a jackpot and make a big production of his achievement.

3. Any interaction with the mat gets clicked and treated. If he leaves the mat, all clicks stop

and you will stand still. If your dog loses complete interest, you will pick up the mat again.

4. Once your dog is consistently offering a *down* on the mat, this is the time to add the cue "mat." So when your dog does a *down*, continue to click and jackpot while also saying, "mat, good mat." And then you will add a release word. For my dogs I say, "Okay." Be sure to stay stationary during the release; say the cue "Okay," then move backwards so he understands that he can get up and move after he hears that cue.

5. After you've cued the release, pick the mat up and begin again.

6. Start rewarding for longer *downs* on the mat. Continue adding your *down* cue while your dog performs a *down* on mat.

7. Once the dog is consistently and strongly performing a *down* on the mat, you've added the release cue for several sessions, and he understands that release means he can get up, then you give the *mat* cue while he's off the mat. If he runs to mat, and you know he understands the cue, move on with the next step in training. If he doesn't run to the mat, continue adding the cue with the behavior as it happens.

8. Start working on distance away from the mat during each session as you cue. Stand one foot from mat and cue it. Click, treat. Next session step back, etc.

9. Start proofing with distractions. Stand one foot away from the dog and throw a neutral object up and down while you cue "mat." Have someone walk by while you cue "mat."

10. Take the mat to different locations.

11. Work on distance in new locations.

12. Work on distractions in new locations.

Go to mat is a great way to maintain control of your dog, and if he were to get loose from you and you were at the pet shop, for example, you can target him to a nearby rug by cueing "go to mat." The *go to mat* can be successfully implemented with any towel, rug, blanket, etc.

It's clear that *go to mat* could be a potentially life-saving command if your dog has a tendency to bolt. As with the *come* command, *go to mat* gives you one more technique in your arsenal to ensure his safety and, if you have a frequent bolter, your sanity.

Stay
Like *go to mat* and *come, stay* is an extremely important cue if bolting is an issue for your dog. You must work on a strong cue so that if the door is opened either to the vehicle or to your house, you can cue "stay," and your dog will be able to have the impulse control to wait until he hears the release cue.

The *stay* cue promotes strong impulse control for your dog and helps him learn to focus. Teaching *stay* will help with the overall program, but you will also use stay while out walking your dog. You may use a *stand* or *sit-stay* before you cross the street, if you need to tie your shoe, and many other times you find yourself needing a strong *stay* behavior.

I teach *stay* a little differently than I originally learned using traditional methods. I prefer to set dogs up for success by not adding the cue first. Rather, I will establish the behavior of *stay* and then add the cue *stay*. This reversal of the traditional order prevents constant corrections. During the process of establishing the *stay* behavior, I will not use the cue *stay*, but I will still use a release cue such as *okay*.

When you first start teaching the behavior of *stay*, you establish the behavior by encouraging duration. Once you've established a 15- second duration, you will start working with distance by having the handler back up.

How to Teach Stay:

1. Cue your dog to "sit." Click when he *sits*. Stand by him and give an occasional treat.

2. Once your dog is able to *sit* with you standing by him for about 15 seconds, then move on to the next step.

3. Start adding movement. Click if your dog stays in a position. Note: If my dog moves into a complete *down* (lying) instead of a *sit*, I find this acceptable.

        a. Rock back and forth. If your dog stays in a *sit* position, click and treat.

b. Pick your feet up as you rock back and forth. If he *stays*, click and treat.

c. Move your feet back and forth in front of dog. If he *stays*, click and treat.

d. Pivot your foot back and forth. If he *stays*, click and treat.

e. Take one full step to the side then the other side.

f. Take one full step back.

g. Take two full steps back.

h. Take a step to the dog's side. If the dog *stays*, click and treat.

i. Step to the dog's other side. If he *stays*, click and treat.

j. Walk around the dog while luring him with a treat in front of his nose.

k. Give your dog your back while you turn your head to maintain eye contact.

l. Dance in front of your dog.

m. Talk in a high-pitched voice.

n. Run up towards your dog.

o. Sing in front of your dog.

p. Give your dog your back and only look back occasionally to build *stay* duration.

q. Walk away, giving your dog your back, but still look back occasionally.

r. Move halfway around your dog.

s. Shift weight and rock in front of him.

t. Move all the way around the dog.

Once the dog is able to *stay* while you move, it is time to add the "stay" cue. I verbally cue this, but I also add the non-verbal cue of my hand flat out in front of the dog's face. You will repeat all the steps listed above, but this time you will add the cue.

Importance of the Release Cue

The release cue is very important and often forgotten. It is imperative to communicate to your dog that he has permission to get out of the *stay* position. When handlers forget to communicate the release cue, dogs are confused or hesitant. Dogs need consistent communication. Be consistent with your release cue no matter what behavior you are releasing because, to your dog, this cue means he will have permission to move around. *Come* is such an important cue and should not be used as a release cue with *stay*. I use *okay* as my release word.

For example, you will cue your dog to "stay," do one of the activities on the pervious page, and then say "okay." As you give the release cue, be sure to remain stationary. The reason for this is, if you move as you say "okay," your dog will learn to watch your body movement rather than learning to listen for the verbal cue. If you move and then say the release word, he will more than likely follow your non-verbal cues.

Cue "stay" → Do one of the activities → Cue verbal release → Move

Following the pattern I have suggested will help you set your dog up for success. After you say the release cue "okay," then you should encourage your dog to get up (by using movement, a kissing sound, snap of fingers, or a hand clap.) Using this method will help your dog to begin associating the behavior of moving out of *stay* position with your release cue (like "okay").

What to Do If Your Dog Breaks Out of *Stay?*
First of all, handlers need to use their skill to read the dog and know how long he *stays*, and give a release cue before that point. To ensure his success, you don't want to push the dog beyond what he can do within a training session. If the dog has already popped up, then go ahead and use the release cue. In the next session, give the release cue for a shorter period in a *stay*.

Once your dog is performing *stay* with consistency, it's time to take it to the doorway and work on opening/shutting the door.

1. Cue your dog to "stay" in a specific area. I would suggest using a comfortable distance from the door (2-3 yards). Make sure that the mat is in a place where your dog can view what is happening at the doorway.

2. Walk to the door. Walk back to your dog, deliver a treat, and then give the release cue. Continue to increase the time that he is cued in a *stay* on the mat before you release.

3. Cue your dog to "stay" in the same area. Walk to the door and wiggle the handle. Walk back to your dog, deliver treats, and then give the release cue. Repeat this exercise 3-4 times.

4. Cue your dog to "stay." Walk to the door and slightly open it. Close the door. Walk back to your dog, deliver treats, and then give the release cue. Repeat this exercise 3-4 times. Be generous with your treats during this step. Continue to increase the amount of space you open the door. Do not move to step 5 until your dog is able to stay with the door completely open.

5. Cue your dog to "stay." Walk to the door open it and leave the door wide open. Return to your dog. Deliver a handful of treats. Repeat this 3-4 times.

6. Cue your dog to "stay." Open the door the width you typically would when someone visits and start talking as if someone is there. Return to your dog. Deliver a handful of treats. Repeat this 3-4 times.

7. Have a family member or friend help with the remaining steps. Have your helper ring the doorbell or knock as a typical visitor to your home. Cue your dog to "stay" in his place and greet the person as you typically would, but have the visitor remain outside. Shut the door and deliver a handful of treats to your dog. Repeat this 3-4 times in the next few days during random times.

8. Have a family member or friend ring the doorbell as in step 7, but this time you open the door all the way for your "company" to come in. During this process it is important to be generous with your treats. Repeat this 3-4 times in the next few days during random times.

9. Maintain practice and reinforcement of this behavior to set your dog up for success.

Prevent Bolting from Car

While you are working on this exercise, please have your dog on a dropped leash for safety purposes.

1. Once your dog has an established *stay*, place him in his typical resting place in the vehicle. Cue a "stay" and release him out of the car to you. Repeat this 3-4 times for 2 sessions.

2. Practice getting in/out of the vehicle and cueing the "stay." Leave the door open after you get out. Repeat this 3-4 times for 2 sessions.

3. Once your dog is successfully and calmly staying, you can begin to add some distractions like a person walking by at a distance or any other thing that you have been having issues with (like another dog on leash). Be sure when you do add distractions that you do so with distance and that your dog is leashed.

4. Take *stay* to the road. Practice your *stays* in different location. The first place can be in your vehicle parked down the road from your home.

Plan ahead, assess, and train. Since *come* is the most important cue that may save your dog's life, it's definitely worth taking time to reevaluate when your dog doesn't comply and also to observe areas of weakness that need to be more focused upon in the training regimen.

I think it is important to understand, and I hope I have sufficiently communicated this point, that sometimes teaching one command leads to the need for teaching another as is the case with *come, stay,* and *go to mat.* Though you need to work on individual skills, in order to have a well-trained dog, at some point the skills must become uniform and work together. I think it's also important to note that one skill may not always do the trick for every dog. Sometimes, you must provide your dog with multiple skills that may accomplish the same objective. Such is the case with *come, stay,* and *go to mat* particularly for dogs that have a tendency to bolt. As always, it is important to know your dog, be his advocate, and always, always, always do what it takes to provide for his safety.

MICHELLE HUNTTING

CHAPTER 9
BUILDING FLUIDITY

From the time I was a little girl, I always wanted to learn ballet. The way they so gracefully move, bringing a story to the music, makes me dream of dancing on stage. For my 30th birthday present, I bought myself some ballet lessons. Thankfully, the 10-year olds in my class were very supportive of me. As I stood at the barre, my classmate that stood half my size praised me for how great I was doing. In return, I let her know how really kind she was.

Let me just say that after two dance classes, I determined that the world's true athletes are dancers. The ballet dancers have to work so hard to master their dance with such fluidity.

Similarly, developing fluidity with your dog's behavior takes time, training, and hard work. It's not something that will come overnight, and just like a ballet dancer, you must continue to stretch and practice or you will lose your form. I can share this truth from experience since I do my leg stretches on the counter while cooking and on the bathroom counter while I am drying my hair. That's dedication, and after almost six months I can finally touch my toes!

I want to help you create the *come* behavior that you desire, and in order to do so, you must prepare and train with your dog on three scenarios, using all three cues: *watch*, *leave it*, and *come* (which is moving toward you). Those three scenarios include distance, distraction, and different environments.

Distance

Practice the cue at a distance from the dog. The trainer will look for a reliable behavior 80% of the time when the dog is close before raising the distance criterion. Once your dog responds reliably to the initial distance, the trainer will start moving a little farther away. For your dog's safety, you can have someone hold a leash or use a long line as you slowly put more distance between you and your dog.

Exercise: Drop a pile of treats to distract your dog, and while he is eating, you can move more of a distance away, gradually increasing.

Other exercises that will help with increased distance are ping pong puppy, the two-person game, and hide and seek (See Chapter 7).

If you will be taking your dog out into the field or working so far away that your dog will not be able to physically hear you, I would suggest whistle training or a vibration collar so the sound of the whistle or the feel of the vibration provides the *come* cue. (Please see chapter 10 for these resources.)

Distraction

The truth is, as humans, we never get distracted... Hmmm...What was I saying? Okay, so maybe sometimes we get distracted. If you, for example, are distracted by the television when your grandma asks you to get her a glass of water, does that mean you don't respect your elder? Or, are you not a good friend if your friend tells you a meeting time that you forget and must ask for again?

Many times we expect our dogs to remain always attentive even though we, as humans, lack that capacity. A dog can get distracted because he wants to get involved with something, like watching a bird or butterfly, or because he lacks impulse control and training.

I don't know about you, but there have been many times where I have responded to a request with, "In a minute." I swear if dogs could talk as they are out in the yard sniffing, that's what they would say. They just need a few more minutes to finish up whatever task they have created for themselves before coming when called.

Distractions happen. Life happens. The best thing that we can do is prepare our dog with pre-established scenarios in order to achieve the best results with recalls (*come*).

Different Environments

I feel like a broken record because I am constantly saying this to my students: *Dogs do not generalize very easily!* This means that you must train in different locations in order for the behavior to become generalized. For dogs to generalize you must train the desired behavior inside the house, in the back and front yard, in/out of your car, down the street, etc. It's not enough for them to learn a command in a single situation.

It's important to slowly progress with this diverse training. In other words, on the first day of generalizing, you don't want to take your dog to the dog park. You want to set him up for success by making sure to match his skill level of distractions with the places that you take him. So, for example, once a dog is performing well in the home, the backyard, the front yard, and in class, it is now time to take the show to the road!

A trainer will begin training cues with different distractions, starting with a less distracting environment and building up to increased distractions. For example, a trainer would take a dog to a coffee shop's patio, then outside of a pet food store, and next, inside a pet food store. It is important for the trainer to be fair and not overwhelm the dog with too many difficult distractions at the beginning.

Before moving to the next level of environment, be sure that the previous location is fluid. In other words, ensure that your dog is responding quickly and at least 80% of the time.

Following is my suggested progression with *come* environments:

- Inside the home
- Exercises through the front door (or most frequently used door)
- Backyard
- Through backyard gate
- Front yard
- Through garage door
- Down the road
- Across the street
- Your car in driveway, side of street, and garage

From here, work in the most frequently visited places whatever they may be.

Distraction Exercises:

Call "come" when
- A friend is continuously petting your dog
- A friend continues to deliver treats
- A friend walks by with a leashed dog

You can tell your friend that your dog is in training so that he/she understands why you are using the cue at these times.

As always, when you are starting to work on the distractions with your dog, it's important to set your dog up for success by not asking too much and always rewarding with something of higher value than whatever he had to walk away from.

CHAPTER 10
WHISTLE AND VIBRATION COLLAR

There are times that you may have your dogs out in the field, on a hike, or in an area where they are allowed to roam at a distance from you. During these times when they are not able to hear you, it is advisable to train with a whistle or, for an even greater distance, a vibration collar. In both of these scenarios, the device will be used as a replacement or an additional cue for the verbal *come.*

Before you start working with the whistle or vibrating collar, you must establish the three pillars with the recall, so make sure that you have mastered the eye contact and *leave it!* exercises before adding this new dimension. I would strongly suggest creating your verbal cue *before* these other forms of a cue.

Essentially what you will be doing is replacing the verbal cue with a sound (whistle) or a feeling (vibration). Utilize all the other tools in this book, but you will do additional training by creating a cue of *come* with whistle or vibration.

Whistle

When I teach a whistle recall, I use a regular whistle, but you could use a dog whistle, specially designed to emit a sound only he can hear. The principles are the same.

Whistle Training

Say your dog's name, and as soon as his neck turns, as he is moving toward you, instead of saying "come," blow the whistle and strongly reinforce (lots of treats) when he arrives. After a few repetitions you will eliminate saying his name and simply whistle.

Tip: Sometimes squatting down can help aid your dog in this process, but quickly fade this motion as it will become part of the cue, and we want to work toward the clean *come* cue at the sound of the whistle.

Beginning Exercise: Allow your dog to get distracted. Say his name and as soon as he moves toward you, whistle. When he gets close, deliver treats.

You can easily apply all the games in Chapter 7 with whistle training, but instead of using the word *come,* you will blow the whistle.

Ping Pong Puppy

As training progresses: You will add distance and distraction with the whistle training as your dog's skills progress.

Multiple Dogs

With multiple dogs you will apply the same principles of working with each dog individually and then adding together.

Demonstrating the 2-Person Game from Chapter 7

Vibration Collar

A vibration collar can be used to cue, in this case the command *come*, with a humane sensation of a vibration around the dog's neck. (No shock is involved!) I find this device to be extremely helpful if I am taking my dogs off leash where they will go out farther than they can hear or see me.

The vibration collar goes on like a regular collar, and you will have a remote control that you can push to vibrate when you are cueing *come*. The range of distance for each collar will be different. Please note: The vibration collar is not meant for every dog as some dogs can be very sensitive, and it's important that the cue *come* always has a positive association. Please be very mindful of your dog's body language.

Obviously the feel of a vibration collar can be "funny" to a dog, so it's important to take time to get him used to it before associating the sensation with the *come* cue. Before you begin using the vibration, get your dog used to wearing the collar by doing the exercises below.

Day 1
Place the collar on; deliver three to four treats; take the collar off. Repeat several times throughout the day.
Day 2
If your dog is comfortable, keep the collar on for

15 minutes throughout the day. Be sure to give many treats during this process.

Day 3

Leave the collar on 30 minutes to 1 hour at a time. Again, be sure to give lots of treats during this time.

Collar with Vibration Exercise: Place the collar on your dog; vibrate the collar and heavily treat. Do five, 30-second sessions for two days.

Day three, you will say your dog's name, and as soon as he turns toward you, mark. Take a few steps back. As he is moving toward you, vibrate the collar and heavily reinforce with treats. Continue this process for four days.

Then, move on to the other *come* exercises detailed in Chapter 7.

Tip: Please be sure to watch his body language and not move too fast. If he still seems uncomfortable with the vibration, then go back to the first exercise of pairing the vibration with treat. Do not move on to the *come* exercises until he is comfortable.

As you progress in training with both of these non-verbal cues, you will add:
- Greater distance between you and your dog
- Distractions

It's important to keep your dog safe during distance training so working with a dropped long line works well so you are able to step quickly on it if need be.

Teaching your dog *come* with either a whistle or vibration collar can be not only a needed tool for some dog/owner relationships but also a lot of fun. The important thing once again is not to get ahead of yourself (or your dog) by moving through the steps until mastery of the initial steps is gained.

CHAPTER 11
MULTIPLE DOGS

Having had a multiple dog household my entire adult life, I have learned from experience, and perhaps you have too, that when multiple dogs accidentally get out of the house, they will go farther away than individually, and for my pack at least, stick together.

It is important for all households with multiple dogs to train the *come* behavior together.

Where to Start
Again, if you want a well-built home, you don't want to start with a weak foundation. The same is true with any learned behavior. You want to make sure that the foundation is strong and doesn't have any weak points before attempting to call multiple dogs together. If you have multiple dogs, each dog must first be trained individually. I didn't take all three of my dogs out together when they were going through their eight-week basic courses. They each received individual time with me during the foundational training time. If you have multiple dogs, begin training each of them individually for three weeks working on the *watch*, *leave it*, and *come* exercises. Take the time now to invest in the foundational skills with each individual dog so that you don't end up having regrets later when you bring them together.

When You Start Adding Together

Once the foundation has been built individually with each dog, we will then add a second dog. When you start working with the two dogs, don't expect the same level of focus and impulse control that you would have individually. You will need to work with both dogs until you reach that desired level.

Multiple Dog Cue

When I train for individual dogs to *come*, I use their name. For example, "Boy, *come!*" However, when I am calling all three of my dogs, I use a multiple dog cue, "Dogs, *come!*"

Exercise: With two or more dogs, you say your multiple dog cue (like "dogs"), and as soon as their heads turn, you will mark and call "come." Heavily reinforce with treats.

Once you have the desired focus and quick response from two, you are ready to add a third dog. You will then alternate the dogs together when adding the new dog.

Using my dogs as an example:

Belle & Morgan → Focused→
Belle & Boy→ Focused →
Morgan & Boy→ Focused →
Boy, Morgan & Belle→ Focused

As always, please be sure to work in a safe environment.

Fluidity
Once you have added all your dogs together, you are now ready to move on to developing the distance and distractions that you already worked on with them individually. You will want to make sure that they are all complying 80% of the time. Once you've reached this level of success, you will take them to different locations.

I would suggest having an assistant for the new locations. Be sure to use your drop lines as a precautionary as you work in the outdoor locations.

Having multiple dogs doesn't have to result in double trouble if you are willing to invest the time to each individual dog before pairing them. Not only will they not cause more trouble, but they will likely provide you with double the fun.

www.DeafDogsRock.com

CHAPTER 12
RECALLS FOR DEAF DOGS
by Christina Lee - DeafDogsRock.com

Training a deaf dog to have a solid recall involves commitment to consistent and lengthy training, along with repetition and rewards through positive reinforcement techniques.

Because a deaf dog must be looking at the handler before he can be recalled, mini sessions of *watch me* training are crucial. This training consists of putting the deaf dog on a leash, having a pocket full of high value treats, and every time the deaf dog makes eye contact with you, marking the correct behavior with an open flash of your hand or a thumbs up sign (instead of the sound of a clicker) and then immediately treat, treat, treat. Repeat often. Start in an environment with little or no distractions. I start inside in my living room and have the deaf dog tethered to me. We practice in different areas of the house with different treats. Many times I will incorporate the *come, sit*, and *wait* commands all at once and then mark all three commands with an open flash of my hand and a treat. This technique keeps my deaf dog from getting bored and also keeps him guessing on when and what treat he will get.

Once the *watch me* training progresses, then you can start mini sessions inside the house for *come*. When I sign *come* to my deaf dogs, I use my hand with two fingers and motion the dog to *come* to me.

Tools you will need for recall training a deaf dog:
- Collar
- 6-foot leash
- 20-or 30-foot long line
- Treat pouch
- High value treats (You can use turkey meatballs or light bologna cut into small pieces.)
- Positive body language ("smile and clap wave," which is putting your hands up in the air and wiggling your fingers while giving a big smile)
- Patience and a consistent training schedule

I first start off only a couple of feet away from my deaf dog and motion the dog to *come* with a *come* sign. When the deaf dog *comes*, I give the dog an open flash of the hand (once again, instead of the sound of a clicker to mark the correct response), and then the pup gets a high value treat as a reward. I repeat this process throughout the day and in several different rooms throughout the house. Always do your recall training with a high value treat or favorite toy, and mix things up so when the dog comes to you, he is in for a nice surprise.

Once my deaf dog in training consistently *comes* to me inside my home, I move our short training sessions to outside our home in order to add outside distractions to our training. I go outside and do short recalls with the deaf dog by just using a 6-foot leash. I let the puppy or dog become distracted by whatever is going on outside and then wiggle the leash, and when the dog turns in my direction and makes eye contact with me, I give the *come* sign. When the dog starts to move in my direction, I SMILE broadly, expressing my pleasure for a job well done. I then give the dog an open flash of my hand to mark the correct response and treat. I also make a big deal of the dog coming to me by doing a "hand wave," which , for a deaf dog, is perceived in the same way as clapping to a hearing dog. I want to be extra demonstrative each time so the deaf dog I am working with knows how happy I am to see him. My body language has to be positive so my deaf dogs will run right to me.

When the deaf dog is consistently coming to me on a leash outside, I add a long line to our training program. A long line is like an extra long leash and comes in different lengths. I purchased a 20-foot line for my deaf dog recall training. (Long lines are available at most pet stores.)

I clip a 20-ft line on my deaf dog and let the dog explore for a while. I also start with mini sessions of *watch me* training outside on the long line, but I start with the deaf dog not going more than 6 to 8 feet away from me. Once the deaf dog is consistently checking in with me, I start giving my sign for *come*. At first I am just a few feet away, but as we continue with our training, I increase the distance.

I practice recall training for several days and sometimes change it up. Sometimes I will run the other direction with the 20-foot line attached and then suddenly turn and give the *come* sign. Deaf dogs are known as "velcro" dogs because they like to be near their humans at all times so recall training with them is fun.

When working with or owning a deaf dog, you must never ever chase the dog if he accidentally comes off the lead. If this happens, your first instinct may be to chase the deaf dog, but what you want to do is run in the opposite direction so the dog will chase you, or you should drop down to the ground. Out of curiosity, dogs cannot resist running up to a person on the ground. They just have to see what a person lying on the ground is up to, and in most cases, both a deaf and hearing dog will run up to a person lying on the ground and lick that person on the face.

If you are working with a deaf dog who gets bored easily like my deaf dog Nitro does, then sometimes when I ask for a *come*, I will also ask for a *sit* and then play a scent game. I will motion to him to *come* to me and then put my closed hands behind my back and slip a treat into one of them. After I choose a hand to hide the treat in, I put both hands in front of him for him to choose which hand is hiding the treat. The dog will put a paw or lick the hand he thinks the treat may be in. By doing this fun "pick-hand-number-one-or-hand-number-two" game, we break the monotony of training by adding some variety to our sessions.

Most deaf dogs get excited when I incorporate a scent game into their training just for fun. Both of my deaf dogs think "it's always good to check in with my mom because she has fun or yummy things for me when I go to her."

You can teach your dog that coming to you quickly will result in good things happening like getting a favorite toy to chase or getting the chance to go explore somewhere.

My next step in recall training is to randomly give the *come* sign even if your deaf dog is engaged in playing with another dog. If you make sure your dog gets a treat just for coming to you at a dog park (Make sure you treat your dog when there are no other dogs around to avoid the possibility of an altercation.), as soon as your dog comes to you, give an open flash of your hand and then a high value treat and a "wave clap." After the dog has come to you and gotten his/her treat, then give him the sign to "go play." It is very important to repeat this training session over and over again so your deaf dog knows if he comes to you, he will get a treat and then be allowed to return to playing with other dogs. I can't tell you how many times I see people with hearing dogs at the dog park, and since the owners of these dogs got into the habit of only calling their dog to them when it was time to leave, their dogs will not come to them ever! I was at the dog park one time, and it took this poor gentleman five hours to catch his dog. The dog did not want to go to him simply because his only association with *come* was the negative experience of having to leave the dog park where he was having fun with other dogs.

Even with a reliable recall, I don't recommend letting a deaf dog off leash in an unfenced area. I know some people let their deaf dogs run around just like hearing dogs, but when you live with a deaf dog, you should be the dog's advocate and take extra precautions to keep the deaf dog safe at all times.

I also have taught Nitro and my other deaf dog Bud the signs for *time to drive home* so they know if I sign this cue to them, they will both sprint to the gate at the dog park and wait for me. As soon as we get into the car, they get a treat. *Time to drive home* is another form of a recall, but it is more specific. This sign tells the dogs it is time to go and get into the car where good things happen.

Also, with deaf dogs, we never punish but always redirect them. When one of my deaf dogs shreds a pillow in the house, sometimes I will put my hands on my hips and give a sad face to let him know of my displeasure. This sign is the extent to which I may "punish" him, which is to say, not at all.

In addition, I have a special sign for both of my deaf dogs to *come to mama*, and I pat my hand on my knee over and over. What that means to both my deaf dogs is no matter what they have done, they can approach me and I will rub them all over. By signaling them in this way, no matter what happens, I have a secret cue that also means *come and everything will be okay*. I truly believe sometimes it is also good to have a backup *come* cue. When Bud gets nervous around strangers at the dog park, sometimes he is so distracted he doesn't even recognize the *come* cue-- that is until I get down low to the ground at his eye level and pat my knee. For some reason he will come one hundred percent of the time when I use this cue because this is my comfort cue, which means if he comes to me, I will soothe and protect him. So I have a direct *come* cue and a *come and I will comfort you* cue.

If you are like me and have hearing and deaf dogs, then I do have a universal cue which works with all six of my dogs. They all know the sign for *treat*. I only use this sign when I need all six hearing and deaf dogs to come to me immediately with no hesitation. When I use the *treat* sign, all six of them come running into the house, and they immediately get an open flash of my hand and a biscuit from the biscuit jar.

Vibration Collar

Some people utilize a vibration collar for *look at me* for a long-distance recall. The vibration collar can be introduced during *watch me* training at the beginning of training, but I prefer to introduce it once the recall training is going well. This way the training is kept simple up to the point the recall is going well. Most of our followers at Deaf Dogs Rock Headquarters have discovered the *watch me* training conditions their deaf dogs to always glance over their shoulder to check in; as a result, we don't use the collars, but I know some people really enjoy using them.

The process of training dogs that are deaf to *come* may present some special challenges, but the process and results can be not only fun but rewarding. As always, with hearing or deaf dogs, it is important that you know your dog, "listen" to him, and act as his advocate.

Photos show deaf dog trainer Bobbie Patterson Wiggins working with her deaf Dogo Argentino puppy Riley on recall at the Deaf Dogs Rock Headquarters in Salem, VA.

MICHELLE HUNTTING

CHAPTER 13
RESOURCES

A perfect recall is unrealistic, but an almost perfect recall is very likely. The best advice as a trainer that I can leave you with at the conclusion of this manual is to take 30 days to establish the *come* cue by doing the exercises. Once it is firmly established, weekly review this cue with your dog. Just like your muscles get weak after not working out for two or more weeks, so will your dog's *come* skills. I want to set you both up for success. Review can be easy! Simply add a few exercises into your everyday life.

Following is a section from my recently published book, *Control on Leash.* I felt it important to include this section because all training, regardless of the subject, requires an intimate relationship with your dog and a sensitivity to his moods and feelings as they are nonverbally communicated to us. A knowledge of your dog's communication is as fundamental to your successfully working together as knowing his name. To maximize your training experience, please take a moment to read this section.

Dog Body Language (From *Control On Leash*)

I think that it would be pretty neat if dogs were able to verbally communicate with us. However, if they could do so, it might take away the magic of our relationship dynamic. Dogs are amazing creatures, and if you learn how and pay careful attention, you will be able to tell what your dog is saying. As humans, we use our words and tone of voice to communicate to other humans. Dogs, however, use their body. We use our bodies as well, but as humans we rely heavily on verbal communication.

Dogs have emotions similar to ours in that they experience happiness, fear, stress, or discomfort. Although, there is so much research to be done in our field to understanding dog body language, understanding how they communicate will greatly benefit your leash walking training program. There are skills in reading dog body language that will come with practice and time.

Displacement Behaviors

The behaviors dogs communicate which say *I feel uncomfortable right now* are called displacement behaviors. Recently, when I drove into the grocery store parking lot, there was a gal waiting to cross from the store front to the parking lot, so I stopped my van. I watched her as she crossed in front of my van. She reached her hand up to her face and scratched. I realized in that moment that I had stared at her long enough to make her feel uncomfortable. In the context of this situation, she didn't have an itch to scratch; she was feeling uncomfortable. Displacement behaviors are normal, but they happen out of context. Some examples would be if a dog were to shake off (as though shaking off imaginary water), even though he's not wet, or if he were to lick his lips even though there was no food around, or yawn when a person pets him roughly. Displacement behaviors are normal in and of themselves, but they happen out of context.

In one of my puppy kindergarten classes, a student complained that her dog kept scratching. She shared with me that she tried a different shampoo, checked for fleas, and made sure her dog was on a good diet, but the puppy was still scratching. I started observing them more carefully to see if I could see what was happening. I noticed that every time the owner cued any behavior the puppy scratched. I explained to the owner that her tone of voice was making her puppy uncomfortable. I encouraged the owner to use a softer tone of voice to cue behavior, and the puppy promptly stopped scratching.

Some Displacement Behaviors:
- Licking the mouth
- Self grooming
- Sniffing the ground
- Scratching
- Turning head to the side
- Shaking off

Photo taken by Renea Dahms

This dog is closing his eyes but he's not sleepy.

Photos by Renea Dahms

On the left the dog is looking concerned, ears are back, and licking lips. The dog to the right is licking lips and turning head away. Both are demonstrating displacement behaviors.

When a pet owner observes these types of behaviors, it's important for the owner to adjust the environment or make the environment look different. This doesn't mean that the dog must be removed from the situation (potentially it could), but it certainly means that the environment needs to be made to look different to the dog. The owner may need to use his body to block the dog's view point, or if a child is petting the dog in a rough manner, the owner may need to help the child learn to pet in a gentler way. It could mean that the owner needs to gain eye contact with the dog to make him feel comfortable.

If any displacement is observed, adjustments need to be made because the next level for a dog would be stress, another topic which we will discuss. "Listen" to your dog because he is constantly communicating to you; it's really a matter of learning to "see" his language.

Dogs Do Experience Stress

Just like us humans, our dogs experience emotions, one of which is stress. It is very important for you to watch his body language to see displacement behaviors as you are out leash walking because if the environment is not adjusted appropriately, he can become stressed.

Some Stress Behaviors:
- Sweaty paws (You will see prints on the floor.)
- Excessive shedding
- Heavy panting
- Dilated pupils
- Holding one paw up (foot pop)
- Frequent blinking or no blinking at all
- Tension in the eyes or mouth (face)
- Stiff body
- Not able to take food

If you notice signs of stress, please remove your dog immediately from the situation and work toward relaxation. This could be as simple as leaving a park and returning to the car for 15 minutes. You could allow your dog to listen to relaxing music like *Through a Dog's Ear* CD.

It's important to be your dog's advocate. Watch his body language and protect him. If you know that he will be uncomfortable, walk away with him. If you observe displacement behavior, then adjust the environment.

Happy Dog

Relaxed and happy dogs will, just like humans, show a softer face and body. You know how tense your muscles get when you are nervous, uncomfortable, or stressed. This is no different for dogs. And when you experience happiness and relaxation, your muscles also relax.

Photo by Renea Dahms

When a dog is relaxed, you will see softness around the eyes, ears, jaw, and overall face. Generally when dogs are happy, they have a nice opened mouth with a gentle pant which shows their rhythm of breathing. If a dog is stressed, his mouth can be closed. What do we do when we are stressed? We hold our breath, and so do dogs. Other times our breathing is heavy. With a happy dog, there is a nice rhythm to the breathing pattern. A happy dog almost looks as though he is smiling. Another sign that your dog is relaxed is if he appears "loosy goosy" with his body. In other words, he is moving around with a "wiggly" body.

Photo by Amber Craig

Also, I think it's worth noting that the tail in and of itself is not a good indicator of the dog's state of emotion. I grew up being taught that if the tail is wagging, the dog is happy. This is not always the case. I have seen dogs with wagging tails attack. It's important to look at the body as a whole. In other words, if the tail is stiff along with the entire body, he is clearly indicating stress. But if the body is stiff and the tail is wagging, I would still assume that there is stress and remove my dog from the environment.

Teaching Come
Regardless of the skill you are trying to teach your dog, I hope you now realize that the foundational skills, though pretty much the same, are vital to the success of your endeavor. In closing, then, I leave you with this thought:

A well-trained dog makes for a happy
dog and a happy owner.

Happy Training!

RESOURCES FOR BOOK

www.kathysdao.com/articles/The_First_Steps_to_Te aching_a_Reliable_Recall.html

The Dog's Mind by Bruce Fogle
Pelham Books, 1990

ADDITIONAL SUGGESTED RESOURCES

Gotta Go! Successfully Potty Train Your Dog by Michelle Huntting

Control on Leash by Michelle Huntting

Dogs Are Gifts from God by Karen Palmer

Plenty in Life is Free by Kathy Sdao

Do as I Do! by Claudia Fugazza

Family Companion Dog by Renea Dahms

"Crate Games for Self-Control and Motivation" DVD

"The Language of Dogs" DVD

SUGGESTED WEBSITES

Kenyon K9 Foundation
www.kenyonk9foundation.org

Kenyon Canine Institute
www.kenyoncanineinstitute.com

Deaf Dogs Rock
www.deafdogsrocks.com

Tellington Touch®
www.ttouch.com

Certified Applied Animal Behaviorist
www.certifiedanimalbehaviorist.com

Dog Bite Prevention
www.doggonesafe.com

Parent Education for Preparing Baby and Dog
www.familypaws.com

Pet Nutrition Information
www.rodneyhabib.com

Through a Dog's Ear
www.throughadogsear.com

MICHELLE HUNTTING

Join on-line group classes
Skype® sessions/phone consults

Phone: 910-583-1924

Email: info@michellehuntting.com

Follow Michelle Huntting:
www.michellehuntting.com
www.missbellesmanners.wordpress.com
www.facebook.com/missbellesschoolfordogs

CPSIA information can be obtained
at www.ICGtesting.com
Printed in the USA
LVOW13s1924201217
560368LV00011B/850/P